Praise for Dave and the Inspirational Book Writer's Retreat (IBWR)

Too many live their life and don't reach their full potential. That was definitely me until Dave and the IBWR team inspired me to UNLEASH! The whole experience was totally life-changing, transformational in fact! From the conventional life coaching approach to the unconventional nuances of heart and soul, IBWR is "THE PLACE" to turn your dreams into reality.
Kelvin Holliday
Founder and Head Adventurer
Transformational Group

The Inspirational Book Writers program is the perfect platform to get your ideas finally out to the world, and your book is by far the greatest business card you can ever design!
Daniel Tonkin
Entrepreneur and Author

IBWR and Dave Thompson have been essential for my personal and professional dream to get a book written. Two years down the track and I have written 5 books with IBWR and have 8 more to easily smash out with this system!
Love working with Dave.
Jean Sheehan
Director Millennium Education
International Speaker and Author

This book is for anyone that knows they are destined for greatness. As Dave says, most people want to play a big game, only a few actually do. This book is for the special individual that is claiming their greatness and sharing it with the world. If you have ever had an idea for a book, this book will lead you to action.

Matt Lavars
Lead Coach & Trainer at The Coaching Institute

"Wow, I haven't stopped crying, you're speaking to my Soul.

Your book is Manna from heaven! A blend of Jedi mind powers with genius pearls of wisdom, and so many #TruthBombs.

Not sure which parts I loved the best? Maybe the warnings to stay away from mental masturbation or how perfectionism is dangerous, maybe even soul destroying!

What I know to be true is - whoever enters the 'IBWR Island' Vortex will be truly blessed, and taken care of like royalty.

Ha! There is no way you can hide because Dave sees all the procrastination tactics, he knows them all!

On a personal note, I've been the recipient of Dave's ability to hold delicious, grounded space, like a BOSS!

Thank you for being a beautiful human.
Arohanui"

Patty-Ann Waho
Intimacy Coach

Dave Thompson has a strategic mind that is nothing short of world class. His coaching ability to navigate the fastest solution to generate the result you want to create is truly spectacular.

In a 10 minute conversation, Dave helped me identify the key words to succinctly sum up the industry niche I'd just newly created. This has not only set the direction of my 1st book but transformed the conversation around my brand and business and opened up a world of opportunity.

The transformational ability of his coaching and strategic mind is what founded the Inspirational Book Writers program and is behind the epic results IBWR continues to create for people in both their personal and business lives.

When working with Dave Thompson and any of his programs, 'breakthrough' and 'transformation' are very accurate words to describe what you will experience.
Justine Davis
Director
Icing Agency

Dave Thompson's Inspirational Book Writers Retreat delivered on every promise. Need a creative and nurturing space to write in? – done. Need support, encouragement, collaboration and challenge to turn your book from a mess of ideas into a finished book? – done. Need to know how to market and launch your book and become an Amazon Best Seller? – done. I always thought it would be hard to write and publish a book. It wasn't. It was far easier than I imagined and it's because Dave and his team make it that way.
Stacey Ashley
Award Winning Coach
LinkedIn Top Voice & Amazon Best Selling Author of The New Leader

My experience with Dave and the team and IBWR was world class. From start to finish, the program is skill fully designed to ensure participants move through the process of book writing with ease and confidence. If you want to write an amazing book in the shortest possible time with the backing of an experienced and supportive team, IBWR is the program of choice.
Salena Kulkarni
CEO&Investment Advisor
Chartered Accountant
Founder of The Freedom Warriors Mastermind

The Book Writer Breakthrough

First published in 2019 by Thompson Coaching Group International Pty Ltd
Brisbane, Queensland, Australia

© Thompson Coaching Group International Pty Ltd

The moral rights of the author have been asserted.

This book is a SpiritCast Network Book.

Author:
    Thompson, Dave

Title:
    The Book Writer Breakthrough; Your Guide For Overcoming The Resistance To Finally Write, Publish & Launch Your Book

ISBN:
    9781730726927

All rights reserved. Except as permitted under the Australian Copyright Act 1968 (for example, a fair dealing for the purposes of study, research, criticism or review), no part of this book may be reproduced, stored in a retrieval system, communicated or transmitted in any form or by any means without prior written permission. All enquiries should be made to the publisher at dave@livingoutrageously.com

Editor-in-chief: Anita Saunders
Cover Design: Bliss Inventive

Disclaimer:
The material in this publication is of the nature of general comment only, and does not represent professional advice. It is not intended to provide specific guidance for particular circumstances and it should not be relied on as the basis for any decision to take action or not take action on any matter which it covers. Readers should obtain professional advice where appropriate, before making any such decision. To the maximum extent permitted by law, the author and publisher disclaim all responsibility and liability to any person, arising directly or indirectly from any person taking or not taking action based on the information in this publication.

The Book Writer Breakthrough

Your Guide For Overcoming The Resistance To Finally Write, Publish & Launch Your Book

Dave Thompson

A SPIRITCAST NETWORK BOOK

There are a million people who want to write a book.
Most don't.

Here's why.

Dedicated to everyone motivated to make an impact and leave a legacy

Table of Contents

Are you ready to breakthrough? 1

Saying YES 7
Imposter Syndrome 9
The "Too Hard" Basket – Overwhelm 15
Strike While The Iron Is Hot – Act Now 21

Write 27
Guided or Solo? 29
Where Do I Even Start? Procrastination 33
Perfectionism 39

Publish 45
Who can help me publish? 47
HOLD THE PRESS! (The Ultimate Sabotage) 51
The Strong Finish 55

Launch 59
The Spotlight 61
The Micro-Celebrity 67
The Rewards 71

Conclusion 77
About Dave Thompson 79
The Book Map Game Plan Session 81
Publish + Launch Program 83
Inspirational Book Writers Retreat 85
Contact Us 87

Chapter 1
Are You Ready To Breakthrough?

"So many people talk a big game. Will you be one of the few that walk their talk?" - Dave Thompson

He was alive with enthusiasm.

"This is the single most important project that will take my life and business to the next level" he said.

I smiled – because I knew it was true.

After 15 years in the coaching game, the last 5 years coaching books, I know when someone needs something, and this guy needed to write his book.

He'd built his business and people were paying attention.

The demand was evident - his fans were asking him every day "when will you write a book?"

His business was growing and in order to reach more people, he really needed products that could leverage his expertise.

The timing was perfect too.

We discussed the timeline of writing, publishing and launching, and we both agreed the time to begin was now.

Everything seemed set – as close to the stars aligning as you can get. I'd seen book writer's start with way less than this guy had; he was a class operator and I knew his book would light up the world when it launched.

But then he unexplainably pulled out.

And that's why I wrote this book.

I'm so passionate about great people with great ideas sharing them with the world, and so this event stirred curiosity in me to investigate the inner world of book writing.

- Why do so many people want to write a book, yet so many hold back?

- What makes people say yes?
- Why is getting started SO DIFFICULT?
- How do you overcome perfectionism, procrastination and self-sabotage?
- Why do so many people write 5,000 words and STOP?
- Why do people get to 95% done, but never complete or launch?
- How come some people take YEARS to write their book?

My investigations led me to discover the 12 major obstacles that stop people from writing, publishing and launching their book. I call this the resistance, and in this book, I will help you overcome it.

My Intention For You

My intention for this book is to shine the light on the obstacles that stop awesome people from writing, publishing and launching their inspirational book to the world.

If you become aware of the pitfalls, you can stay on the book writing path and actually publish and launch the book.

Because if you are reading this, I know you are a leader in your field, with a lot of wisdom to give. Your special talents, unique skills, and transformative abilities can really make an impact for people.

You can solve their problems.

You can uplift them with your story.

You can raise the consciousness of the planet with your revolutionary approach.

BOOKS = IMPACT.

BOOKS = LEGACY.

Of course, you'll get the credibility of being an acknowledged authority, and tailor the book launch to bring in new leads, fresh opportunities and open the door to international keynote speaking. These are a given.

But I know it's THE IMPACT and THE LEGACY that you really came for, what you really want.

How to Read This Book

I've divided this book into 4 pieces:

SAYING YES
WRITE
PUBLISH
LAUNCH

In each piece, I'll talk about the major obstacles I've seen play out in the book writers I've coached over the last 5 years. Some obstacles could have appeared in any or all pieces, but I just grouped them for ease of reference, and based on my experience.

You can start from the beginning and read cover to cover, or just flip to the topic you that most effects you.

What Next?

Maybe you've recognized yourself in some of the patterns mentioned in this book. If so, I hope the following pages help to breakthrough.

Please do let me know, as I'd love to celebrate your successes with you.

You can email me on dave@livingoutrageously.com

And, if you've loved this book, I'd really appreciate it if you left an awesome review on Amazon, or email me and tell me what you thought, or even share it with a friend who wants to write a book.

Chapter 2
Saying Yes

"Say Yes – And Then Figure Out How"

Imposter Syndrome

"I have written 11 books, but each time I think, 'Uh oh, they're going to find out now. I've run a game on everybody, and they're going to find me out."

- Maya Angelou

Imposter Syndrome is one of the first big obstacles to overcome when writing, publishing and launching your book. I get it – you're stepping up – and doing something new – outside your comfort zone.

You're used to your day-to-day activities, you're used to your current level of authority, fame, and power, and all of a sudden you are doing something that will take you to the next level – to micro-celebrity and beyond. Everyone talks about the next level – but the truth is it can cause a mini-freak out when you get there.

Left unchecked, Imposter Syndrome will stop you in your book writing tracks, freezing your flow and placing an indefinite pause on your plans to get your ideas out into the world.

It's caused MANY people to give up.

But I know you're not the type to do that.

So let's look under the hood into what exactly Imposter Syndrome is, why it happens, and what you can do about it.

Wikipedia[1] defines Imposter Syndrome as: *a psychological pattern in which an individual doubts their accomplishments and has a persistent internalized fear of being exposed as a "fraud".*

It can be readily identified when you hear people say things like:

"Who am I to write a book?"

"Only experts write books, but I'm no expert!"

"No one wants to read what I've got to say!"

"I'm a crap writer!"

"If I write a book, people will finally find out I'm a charlatan/fake/cult leader and I'll be chased out of town!"

Ok – maybe you haven't heard someone say the last one, but I'm sure you can relate to the sentiment.

In tribal times, being chased out of town was NOT good. You'd be lost, alone in the wilderness, having to fend for yourself. Without modern technologies, surviving outside of your tribe was tough, and probably meant an early death. Which means that somewhere, deep in our modern 21st century unconscious mind, is this reptilian voice that says:

"DON'T BE AN IMPOSTER OTHERWISE THEY'LL CHASE YOU OUT OF TOWN AND YOU'LL DIE".

Thus, to the reptilian brain that wants to keep you safe, book writing looks risky.

But is it true?

OF COURSE IT'S NOT TRUE!

Let's talk real for a second.

---

[1] https://en.wikipedia.org/wiki/Impostor_syndrome

If you're out there big noting yourself, and inflating your abilities, but then can't deliver – then yes – you are an imposter. Misrepresentation is not cool, and there's a whole section in the *Trade Practices Act* about the bad stuff that happens to people who make misrepresentations in business.

But if you're reading this book, I know that's not you. I know you're a person of integrity, who has actually lived what you're writing about. I also know that when it comes to delivery, you deliver, and then some!

So let's stop this non-sense about Imposter Syndrome.

Here's how.

1. Quit Focusing On Yourself

Imposter Syndrome rears its ugly head when you are focusing more on yourself than on your purpose and mission for the book. When you make it all about you, you are inviting in self doubt and questions around self worth.

Stop it!

You started this journey because you had something you wanted to contribute to the world – something of value – that can inspire people, solve problems, and raise the consciousness of the planet.

Think about all the great books that have changed your life. For me in this book business, the thoughts of Seth Godin have been particularly profound. Without the influence of his thinking, this book program would be completely different, and it certainly wouldn't exist in its current format. Interestingly, even Seth faces Imposter Syndrome! He writes about his experiences with it in one of his books.

Your words have the power to inspire, heal, transform, entertain, educate and enlighten. Given all the issues going on globally, I believe it is your obligation, as a leader in your field, to share your knowledge.

Don't make it about you.

Make it about what you can contribute, and how you can help.

2. Quit Comparing Yourself To Others

Comparison.

It's so tempting, and social media makes it so easy to compare your life and business to everyone else's life and business. When you're stuck hustling to make ends meet, and Facebook is full of friends on vacation in overwater bungalows in the Maldives, it can be disheartening.

Realise that social media is everyone's highlight reel. Few people share the dark times, the failures or the times when it just got plain weird.

An alternative approach, if you must compare, is to compare yourself against yourself. For example, if you've tried for 7 years to write your book, and now you are actually writing it, WOHOOO!! Progress!!

The best approach though – just quit comparing yourself to anyone or anything, and focus on the present moment on what you want to create – which is an outstanding book.

3. Bench Your Inner Critic

High achievers are often quite hard on themselves. Often its part of their success strategy.

If you let the inner critic run wild, he or she will go searching, and inevitably find something that's not perfect, triggering off feelings of being a fraud.

Give your inner critic a chill pill, and sit him on the bench, we won't need his services for this one.

4. Realize That No One Has Their Shit Figured Out

One of the most liberating things to know is that literally every single person on the planet is making things up as they go along. I am literally making up the words in this book, right now, as I type. Look, I made up more words!

You don't have to have everything figured out, and it is ok to make things up on the spot. I had a mentor once who ran a multi-million dollar business. When asked a question, he would say "well, there's 2 things about that", pause for a few seconds while he thought of 2 things to answer with, and then say "number 1 – XYZ, number 2 – ABC"! He was just buying himself time!

School teaches us to memorise answers, to have them pre-loaded and ready to go. But this is not school, it's real life. No one has got their shit figured out, it's just the ones who are brave enough to have a go, that end up creating amazing things in the world.

5. Your Authentic Voice Is Valuable

People want to hear from you! They want to hear a unique voice, speaking to their hearts and souls in real language they can understand. They want your unique flavor, your unique values, and your unique beliefs. They don't want a carbon copy of Tim Ferris; they want what I call an "authentic original".

An authentic original is something that is not mass-produced for the mainstream. It is something that is written and created by a unique person, who is infusing their uniqueness, in order to help a specific niche of people. Your book is your brand, and it's a tool to attract ravings fans, and have people who are not your fans, opt-out! This is good, because you want to polarize your audience so they opt-in hard and say "she's my girl!"

The way to do this is through owning your authentic voice. I have had several clients who failed high school English come through the book program. All of them were worried about being found out as a fake. What I coached them to do, was to own their voice. They didn't try to make things complicated, or overlay 25 maps and models over their writing. They chose simple, clean communication as their mode of delivery, and told their readers that's how it would be in the introduction to their book.

Your voice is your competitive advantage.

It's what cuts through the noise.

And so when it comes to book writing, as book writer Benjamin Reeves would say, JUST DO YOU.

6. Be Honest

Have you ever seen a pop star get grilled in the media for lip-syncing? Why does everyone give them such a hard time? It's because they were actually faking it, and got found out. It would have been so much easier to just say at the top of the performance: "hey guys, so, I'm going to be dancing up a storm for you all to this song, and so singing at the same time is going to be quite hard, so I'm going to lip-sync for you, just wanted to be transparent and let you know."

An honest statement like that encourages so much trust in the audience. The other thing it does, is it makes the star seem human, which comes in handy should heaven forbid they make a mistake and be seen to be not perfect.

People are far more forgiving to transparent, honest people.

In book writing – don't try and make your voice something it is not.

So, be honest with your intentions, and with your style, tell people in the introduction what they are going to get – and ask for permission for your writing style!

A line at the top of the book saying, "This book is written in my normal dynamic, conversational tone, and yes, we will move fast" will do wonders for engendering more trust in your reader.

The Too Hard Basket Overwhelm

Standing at the foot of the jungle, they saw 4000 feet of vertical rise (that's a lot!), an overgrown jungle canopy that was seemingly impenetrable, and a single solo male returning from the summit. The man was sweating profusely, had a scary looking beard and his clothes were torn, it looked like he had been through ALOT— it just looked hard!

Writing a book is a lot like going on a hiking expedition. When you set out for the first time, it can seem like the jungle mentioned above, and no one wants to be that sweaty man! As a result, many quit before taking even one step.

It just LOOKS hard.

I can see why. There are 185 items on our internal company publishing checklist for each book. Without a guide, this could be overwhelming to navigate.

Of the 185 tasks to complete for each book — none are particularly challenging — but if you didn't know what the steps were, you'd spend hours if not days or weeks just trying to work out where to put your foot next.

Csikszentmihalyi, in his book on *Flow*, said that a flow-state happens when the task at hand challenges the abilities of the person. If it is too difficult, it becomes burdensome, and flow does not happen. If it is too easy, it becomes boring, and flow does not happen.

Book writing is frequently perceived as being too difficult. Therefore, without adequate support, it's hard for you to get into flow with the task of book writing and that's why so many get overwhelmed.

With so many tasks to complete in a book writing journey, you need support to guide you so you can stay in flow.

Here's a short list of some of the tasks involved in writing, publishing and launching a book:

- Deciding on a title and sub-title combination that will both sell books and accurately tell the reader what your book is about
- Be structured in such a way that grabs the reader's attention from the first page (seriously you must get buy-in on the first page, otherwise they may be gone forever)
- How to effectively marry the competing desires of giving value, while also selling your program/service
- Acquire International Standard Barcode Numbers, or ISBNs
- Finding quality service providers for editing, formatting and cover design
- Finding a printer that doesn't demand you print 5000 copies straight up.
- Copyright, disclaimers and other legal considerations
- What article of the tax treaty do I quote, to ensure I don't pay Uncle Sam more tax than I have to, on amazon sales?
- Speaking of Amazon, how do I even make that happen?

The truth is, there's a lot to writing, publishing and launching a book. There are so many tasks. This is the reality.

And what with work, clients, relationships, kids, sports, dishes – life can full.

And - not everyone has 6 months spare to go sit in a villa in Bali and write their memoirs.

So, what can we do?

1. Pause The Belief That It Is Hard

The belief that writing a book will be hard has stopped many book writers in their tracks. They hear the hard stories and believe them to be true. Don't do that!

Yes – I'll be straight with you – book writing can be hard at times. Like any summit attempt, there are sections to navigate that can be challenging. And yes, a fairly big chunk of brainpower is often required to write a book.

But it doesn't all have to be slog and grind. So many of the inspirational book writers who join us on our island retreats surprise themselves with how easy it is.

As one of our clients said on the final day of a recent book retreat, "the remarkable thing is, it was so easy."

What if your book could be written with grace and ease? What if it was an enjoyable experience? What if the heavy lifting was taken off your hands, and you just focused on what you do best?

How would that feel?

2. Pause The Belief That It Takes Forever

I think a lot of people put writing a book in the too hard basket because they believe it will take them many months, if not years. With the fast paced, dynamic world we live in, it's harder for people to commit to a process that could take 18, 24 or 36 months.

The truth is, book writing will take as long as you allow it to take.

Our first ever book writer, leadership coach Michele Jones, had her book written and published, and in her hot little hands, within 42 days of first putting pen to paper! Now, that included 10 days for shipping!

At the Inspirational Book Writers Program, we use the famous Parkinson's Law to help us get our books done.

Parkinson's law states that the size of a task will swell or shrink according to the amount of time allocated to it.

So, if you have a school assignment and are given all term to do it, it will often get done in the final week. The same as if you were given a week to complete it, you'd narrow your focus onto the mission critical items, and get it done in the week.

On our book retreats, our writers have 7 days to complete their book – but often they are finished much earlier.

Some, like Jean Sheehan and Kelvin Holliday, finished their first books by Day 3, and so decided to use the rest of the time to write a 2nd book! All power to you guys!

So, book writing does not have to take forever, in fact, one of our book writers is planning on writing 5 books in 5 days on retreat next year!

3. Get An Experienced Guide To Show You The Shortcuts

The journey of book writing is full of micro-decisions.

"Do I put this story in chapter 2, or chapter 6?"

"Do I go into that much depth on that model, or just give them the big pieces?

"Should I tell that story? What will my [insert family member of choice] think?"

I've known people to have their book writing mission put on indefinite pause, because they stopped at one of these micro-decisions, and didn't know how to proceed. Other times, they have to stop, do research and think about how they will proceed – this can take hours, day, months, or years.

Having an experienced guide helps you to quickly move through these micro-decisions with grace and ease and flow, allowing you to keep your momentum high. One of the rules we have on the Inspirational Book Writers Retreat is that if you have stopped for more than 60 seconds on any micro-decision, then put your hand up and get help.

The help might just be asking for a soundboard to bounce ideas off. It might be a strategic conversation about the direction or structure of the writing. Or it might be you need some moral support – a cup of tea and chat often goes a long way to getting you back on track.

4. Focus On One Thing At A Time

Writing a book is a lot like eating an elephant, it's not going to happen unless you just take one bite a time.

When I wrote my first book many years ago, I had no idea how to start. It just seemed far too hard. I turned to my friend, Matt Kelly, who had written a book on Outsourcing the previous year to ask him how to do it.

Matt Kelly said, "Dude, you need to focus on one thing at a time. When I wrote my first book, I asked myself, ok, what do I first need for a book?

The answer: words.

So I wrote words.

Great.

Now what do I need?

Editing.

Who can edit for me?

Found someone. Great.

Now what do I need?

And I continued this process of asking myself Now what do I need? Until I literally had the published book in my hands."

Focussing on one task at a time reduces overwhelm, puts you into action and builds momentum towards a finished book.

5. Immerse Yourself In The Task of Book Writing

I know some people tout the idea of a disciplined 30 minutes of writing a day, and over the course of a year you get your book done.

But seriously, who is that disciplined, and who wants to wait a year?

What I've found works far more effectively, is to immerse yourself in the book writing for large chunks of time, preferably a block of days.

This works for several reasons. One, there is what I call, "brain start up time" to consider. When I start writing, I often spend the first 15 minutes reviewing what I've already written, reviewing notes and such, to "switch on" and "warm up" my brain to the task of writing.

Two, immersion creates flow and momentum and productivity. It does that, because as humans, we only have a limited number of chunks of attention. When we immerse in the task, we can dedicate our full attention to the book, which often shortens the amount of time required to complete it. It's kind of like trying to do a school assignment while also texting your friends, cooking dinner, updating your social media and watching The Bachelor – your focus is skewed everywhere and it will cause the amount of time it takes to complete to drag out considerably.

Much better to get in, give the book your full attention for a short period of time, get it done and then get out again and continue on with your life.

Strike While The Iron is Hot Act Now!

The following conversation was between myself and a very good friend and client of mine, Dane Tomas. He has published stacks of books with us and the text exchange below shows how quickly he acted on an idea.

August 5th

Dane: "yo bro…guess what? i'm writing another book "Secrets of a Sex Wizard"

Dave: "epic! When did you have the idea?"

Dane: "last night"

Dave: "so good!"

Dane: "can we have it printed by September 6th? I've got workshop gig in Melbourne I want bring the book to."

Dave: "sure thing, we'd need all the stuff done by August 22nd though!"

Dane: "I'm already 12,000 words deep."

Dave: "well lets get book number 5 rolling then!"

Often, like Dane, you will know in your heart of hearts when it is time to write your book. They are the kind of things that just don't go away, until, the day they do…

Follow me here...

If there is one thing I've learnt while coaching books for the last 5 years and having written 5 books myself (this is #6), it's that when the idea is fresh – that's the time to strike.

Creativity is like a good woman.

If you ignore her, she ain't going to hang round very long.

So – if your book idea is knocking you in the face – act on it.

NOW.

Otherwise, just like the good woman, she will go find someone who WANTS to play with her.

And when you find out a colleague wrote about the exact ideas you were about to write about, you will realize the truth in my words.

Just ask Elizabeth Gilbert, famous for *Eat Prey Love*. She had an idea for a new book, got started, got deep in the process, but then life got busy and she parked it for 18 months. By the time she got back to it, she discovered, much to her dismay, that a colleague of hers had written about her EXACT idea and that book was now published! (Check out her new book *BIG MAGIC* for more on this story).

If you continue to put off writing your book, a couple of things can happen:

1. The idea leaves you, and someone else gets all the credit for a revolutionary new idea in your space.
2. The ambitious up-and-comer in your industry starts to gain traction ahead of you, because they were nimble and fast and brought a book to market before you.
3. You run out of time and life moves on, without your book. We often work with people who are just about to have a baby, just about to move overseas, or have for whatever reason just found themselves with a large chunk of available time (sometimes through recovery from a health operation or similar). If you've

got the available time, do it, because when the next season of your life rolls around, you will be too busy to make it happen.

So, what can we do about it?

1. Did The Dog Really Eat Your Homework?

To help you strike while the iron is hot and your idea is fresh, it pays to take a quick look at what excuses you have you been using for not writing your book.

So, what's your excuse?

And – is it true?

The reality is there are probably some valid reasons why you haven't done it yet, and also a stack of reasons that are just socially acceptable justifications for putting it off.

So, what's your excuse?

And – is it true?

2. How Long Have You Wanted To Write A Book?

I've met people who have wanted to write their book for 35 years. One client of the book writers program first had their idea in college as a 20 year old, and he was 55 when he finally wrote the book on his idea. Fortunately, his idea hadn't left him over all that time!

What I've noticed is that prospective book writers follow a typical pattern, that can be explained by reference to the hero's journey. The hero's journey is a story-telling framework that is used by almost all successful Hollywood movies.

The hero acknowledges the need to change and evolve, and goes up to the precipice, about to accept the call to adventure and plunge head first into the next level of his life and business. But then, at the last moment, he pulls out, shrinking back into his shell.

He has refused the call to adventure.

But that's ok, because I'm telling you, its part of a predictable cycle.

Because soon enough, the pressure will build up again for him to breakthrough, and this time HE WILL ACCEPT THE CALL TO ADVENTURE.

When he says yes this time, THIS is when the new world begins.

So, in the spirit of continuing to get real with ourselves, how long have you wanted to write your book?

In full transparency, for me, I'd wanted to write this book for 5 months. I was going to write it at the June 2018 Inspirational Book Writer's Retreat, but then that retreat sold out. When a space became available on the October 2018 book retreat, I was like BOOM! I'm in!

3. Get Clear On What Are You Actually Saying Yes To?

Agreeing to write a book can be a lot like agreeing to marriage and kids – you know you want it, but you don't quite know what you are getting yourself into.

That's why it is useful to clarify exactly what you are saying yes to, when you pull the trigger and decide to write your inspirational book.

There is a uniquely different answer for each person, but here are some common themes that I've seen book writers mention.

From a metaphorical point of view, you're agreeing to a couple of things:

It's a line in the sand: You've been on a journey in your life and business, you faced the tests, challenges and enemies, and you've come out the other side with unique special wisdom. You're ready to use that special wisdom in the next phase of your life and business, but first you want to capture that wisdom in a book.

To that end, its like drawing a line in the sand, proclaiming the past to be the past, acknowledging that you've learnt so much during that period, and that you are ready to step forward into the bright new future. This is particularly the case for inspirational life story with lessons type books but also for business how to books.

It's you staking your claim: Publishing a book is a lot like staking your claim for your position in the marketplace.

It's a statement that says: THIS IS WHAT I STAND FOR.

It's like building a lighthouse, and then turning on the light, so all those who need your help can find you.

It's a decision to be the authority in your space: To be acknowledged as the authority in your space, you really need to own the fact that you know your stuff. If you aren't confident, or a bit blasé about what you know, you can't expect the marketplace to agree you are the authority.

What often happens during the book writing journey is there is a moment of recognition for each book writer, when they realize just how much they know, and how valuable that is.

IT'S TIME.

LET'S START WRITING.

Chapter 3
Writing It

"Everybody said, SAY SOMETHING."
– lyrics from Justin Timberlake's latest song

Guided or Solo?

This is the first fork in the road when beginning the journey to writing, publishing and launching your inspirational book.

Let's look at your options.

Firstly, let's look at going solo in the book writing journey. To be honest, I'd only ever go this route if I was dead broke and literally could not get any money together to pay for help.

When you go solo, EVERYTHING is on you.

Planning the book, writing it, editing it, getting cover designs done, finding formatters to get it ready for Amazon – literally everything is on YOU.

Sure you can ask friends to help – and by a miracle you may have a friend who is particularly skilled in one department who can help you out – but by and large, when it comes to support, you get what you pay for. You pay peanuts, you get monkeys, as they say.

There are a large number of book projects that never got off the ground because someone got negative feedback from a (secretly) jealous friend and took that feedback seriously and so became disheartened and quit. You must be conscious of who you get to give you feedback.

Now, I don't want to dissuade anyone from a solo book writing mission. All power to you. Just be prepared for a VERY steep learning curve, and stay persistent and hungry for the answers – you'll get there – eventually.

Kind of an in-between solo and guided book writing mission is buying a course (usually online) that teaches you what to do. These range from free to cheap to many thousands of dollars, and some are excellent while others are not. I see this option as like having a 2D paper map. It is better than nothing, but still won't give you the peculiarities of your particular book writing expedition.

Guided book writing expeditions are my favourite. I think they rock the most because the best ones blend a "done with you" and "done for you" approach. At no point are you on your own! This allows you to speed up your journey, and address questions as they arise, and keep the momentum flowing. They are definitely the option for the time-poor, results orientated high achiever.

When it comes to guided book writing expeditions, there's a couple of ways you can go:

1. Publish And Launch Packages

These types of packages are particularly great for accomplished writers, who are experienced in writing, or perhaps have written books in the past. You've got a manuscript, and you need help tying it all together – getting a second opinion to check you've covered everything, get help with editing and tidying/polishing the manuscript, interior formatting and layout, and cover designs, distribution on Amazon and printing.

In addition, look for a package that has a proven launch strategy that you can use to launch your book. Producing an amazing book is a bit of a waste if you don't optimize your launch. A good publisher can help you with all of the above.

2. Go On A Book Writing Retreat

The best book writing retreats will handle everything for you, so you can purely focus on getting the book done. They will pick you up from the airport so you don't need to think about transport, feed you amazing delicious food so you don't have to worry about cooking or running out of fuel, and be in a beautiful natural paradise, so you don't need to worry about the distractions of modern life.

Another thing that we really value on our book retreats is completion. You want the culture of the retreat to be one geared around excellence and completion. Going away and not getting it done is called a holiday, and you can take them anytime. Ask your book writing retreat facilitator do they emphasise completion, because if they don't, that means you'll have to go home and finish the book – which can be a lot harder because you're not in the creative environment.

Now that you know what to look for in a program, here's a word on ghostwriting and audio transcriptions.

Ghost writing means paying for someone else to write your book. Typically, you would be interviewed on the phone for many hours, asked questions about your work, and then another writer turns your answers into a book. Initially it appeals to people who think it's an "easy" way to get their book done. And while it can be an effective method for some, what I've noticed is that you, the author, often have to go back through the manuscript, and rework considerable sections to make it sound like it's your voice.

And that's the inherent problem with ghost writing – because someone else is actually writing the book, it's not actually your voice. Authenticity is lost.

And don't even bother with a cheap ghostwriter. The quality will leave you embarrassed and wanting to completely re-work the manuscript.

A good ghost writer can be a solution, but they can be expensive. I know one service provider in the book writing industry that offers a ghost writing service, but charges $100,000 USD.

Overall, it is probably not the best option, particularly if authenticity of voice is important to you.

The audio transcription method on first glance is particularly appealing to people who are good at talking. I actually tried to write my first book by doing audio recordings, and then transcribing them.

Now, I'm sure there is a way to make it work, but I certainty couldn't find it! My attempts at audio produced a large amount of a jumbled mess. It took me HOURS to edit that mess, and eventually I gave up.

You see the thing is, to nail an audio-transcribed book, you REALLY need to know your material, and it needs to come out of your mouth in a very structured, orderly process. If it doesn't and you are all over the place, then you will need to spend so much time on the tail end fixing it up.

For me – this was a deal breaker. I quit the audio method, and I don't recommend it to my clients.

If a client does want to voice record, what we recommend they do is voice record their thoughts as they happen, in the lead up to writing the book. You might be in the yard gardening, taking the kids to school, or just got out of swimming in the ocean when an idea strikes you. In those moments, whip out your smart phone and record your voice message. Have that transcribed, and use THAT as source material for your book. Consider it more like notes, than actual writing.

A Final Note: Don't Skimp On The Cover Design

A picture tells a thousand stories, and a cover tells you so much about a book. Is it cheap and tacky, or does the cover accurately represent the brand and message it is portraying?

We spend a lot of time and money on our covers, using one of the best cover designers in the business. We want the cover to be unique, to pop, to stand out from the crowd while honouring the message of the book and representing the client's brand.

Some book publishers use cheap and tacky cover designers from Fiverr, and the result is cheap and tacky. I don't think that looks good for your brand.

Go with a provider that has a track record of amazing cover designs.

Where Do I Even Start? Procrastination

"What – do I just sit down and start writing?"

It's easy to let procrastination take over when you embark on the book writing journey. For some, procrastination sets in before they even take one step. The mere thought of writing a book causes them to head to the fridge, pull out the chocolate fudge, and get distracted with Netflix.

For the disciplined few that do manage to sit themselves down and open the computer, starting to write a book can be akin to trying to learn to swim butterfly – they're expending a lot of energy, but not really getting too far.

This is frustrating.

Especially for high-achievers, who really don't want to waste their time or energy going round in circles. You'd rather get in and get it done. Smash it out, and move on. Next mountain!

Not to mention the fact that stalling before you've even taken off can be quite embarrassing! If you announce to the world you're writing a book (because, like, public accountability motivates you, right?), then you want to be making progress. You want to be able to proudly tell your colleagues at your next networking event, "I'm writing a book".

So let's say you've started writing.

You've sat down. Opened the computer, and have actually got some words on the page! Wohoo!! Go You!!

Beware of the phenomenon I call "Stuck at 5K".

This is typically the person that set off with the best intentions and full of enthusiasm, but without a plan, or a structure, or support. They get 5000 words in (or maybe 10 or 15 thousand) and then STOP.

Doubt takes over, and the monkey mind runs wild!

"Am I doing it right?"

"Did what I wrote even make sense?"

"Is the writing actually achieving my purpose, or am I just waffling?"

You're so "IN" the writing, it is hard to get perspective on what you're actually doing. It's kind of like the athlete, who makes the same mistake 6 times in a row, until the coach in the box sends him a message, and he course corrects.

Without a coach, it is easy to spiral into uncertainty and distraction.

I've seen some of the most high achieving individuals become Professional Procrastinators, when charged with the task of editing their book.

So what causes procrastination in the book writing process?

From my experience, it comes down to a couple of things:

1. Not Knowing What To Focus On Next

As mentioned elsewhere in this book, our internal company checklist lists 185 items that must be completed per book. If you don't know what to focus on next, it can be easier just to eat coconut ice cream (salted caramel of course) and watch Netflix.

One of the checklists we use in the Inspirational Book Writers program is The Book Content Checklist™. This checklist will guide you on what to do next. If you'd like to get it for free, just head to www.inspirationalbookwritersretreat.com.au/downloads to get your free checklist.

2. Fear Of Actually Getting It Done

Sometimes people know EXACTLY what they need to write next, but they procrastinate around doing it because they are uncertain about what is going to happen once they've written it. Often the pattern is; when faced with the unknown, it is better to do nothing - kind of like animals that play dead when a predator arrives.

3. Negative Feedback From People Who Have No Idea

I've also seen people stall their book writing journey because they received harsh negative feedback from a supposed "friend". Let's be clear — every man and his dog will have an opinion about your book. Getting feedback from the wrong person, who isn't qualified to speak about book writing, can be quite disheartening, and stall a book. So — be selective — and only get feedback from people close to you, and those who you trust. And even then, realize that they will be giving you feedback through their filter of their life experience — so take it all with a grain of salt.

So, what are the keys to overcoming procrastination?

1. Environment Built For Writing Success

Most people try to write their book in their office, at the start or end of a long day. A small percentage will be successful, but most won't. Modern life, and modern environments are boxy, concrete and full of Wi-Fi signals.

Writing is about expression, and to get a natural voice, you need a natural environment.

Personally, I prefer being nearby the ocean, a bay or a lake, because it has a gentle flow. I also like locations that have a distinctly grounded, earthy feel. This is helpful for actually taking the action, turning ideas into pages on a book and actually getting it done. And thirdly, I like areas that have a little bit of fiery energy. Fire encourages passion, and a get-it-done vibe — both are which are conducive to writing books.

Like I've mentioned before, a fully supported space, with a culture of completion, is also important.

2. Accountability

There are SO many opportunities in book writing to quit. Something gets a little bit hard, and you check Instagram, or go see what's in the fridge, or look out the window, or go do something easier.

The resistance is real, and that's why even the most disciplined book writers value accountability. In the Inspirational Book Writers program, we work in 90 minute blocks, checking in on progress so the momentum is maintained.

When a coach sees you reaching for that extra raw dessert, or sees your status come up on social media as "active", he knows procrastination is in town, and can help you stay on task.

3. Direction On What To Do Next

As mentioned above, procrastination sets in when you don't know what to do next.

It's important that you have a Book Map for how you are going to complete your book. Without a map, the temptations of distraction can sway even the most focused book writer. Your book map should be clear and concise, and note your book's purpose, your vision, its message, the structure, target market, voice, and tone.

When getting started writing a book, the introduction is actually one of the most critical pieces. Your introduction needs to be compelling, or else the reader will opt out. The key to having an addictive introduction is all in how you frame up the book.

If you want to learn how to write a powerful introduction to your book, go to www.inspirationalbookwritersretreat.com.au/downloads where you can download the free video and worksheet we use with all our clients, called The Pre-Frame Introduction Builder.

4. Play Your Own Game

Procrastination often sets in when you're trying to play someone else's game.

And I get it – it's your first book – you have no idea how to do it – so you are modeling someone who has done it before. On the surface, this appears to be a great approach. But what if their strategy doesn't suit you?

For example, we once had a client from Sydney who runs a multi-million dollar marketing business. He had a big team of people and multiple times a week, he would be in front of them, delivering speeches. He wrote these speeches on his iPhone, in the notes section.

He was concerned that he wouldn't be very productive on a laptop, typing his book. He was thinking he would be slow, and it would take forever.

When I asked him how he was most productive, he talked about how fast he could prepare a speech on his iPhone.

It was clear that writing on his iPhone was a very productive strategy, and so he wrote the majority of his book on his iPhone, and then transferred it to a word document.

Do what works for you – play your own game.

Perfectionism

Perfectionism is the dragon that has put many a book writing journey on indefinite pause. Perfectionism is defined as a personality trait of striving for a flawless outcome, and being super critical if it's not flawless.

But the thing is – for much of the book writing journey – your book is going to be far from perfect, in fact, it will probably be the opposite.

When you first start expressing your writing, it will probably be clunky and chunky. It might be really dry and logical, or perhaps overly fluffy. You might ram home the point, or not emphasise the point enough, or sometimes, you'll even miss the point!

Being critical of your first attempts at book writing is like criticizing a baby for not being able to drive a car, or lift 100kg! It's crazy, but we do it!

In my experience, everyone feels the dragon of perfectionism at least to some extent. If you love pretty things, love things being in order, and/or have OCD tendencies, then you will probably feel it more so. My job here is to make you aware of how perfectionism is playing out and what it might cost you, and then – what we can do about it.

The costs of perfectionism are high. In the quest to get it perfect, the book writer gets nothing, or very little done. It is a frustrating path of 3 steps forward, one step back. The perfectionist writes one sentence, reviews it, changes a word, deletes it, and re-writes it. It takes 4 hours for one paragraph to be written, and the perfectionist takes this as standard, calculating that at that rate, their book will take YEARS to write.

Then, if you repeat those patterns a few times, it can lead you to doubt the validity of your book, doubt your own confidence, and puts into question whether you have what it takes to write the book.

For the aware high-achievers who know perfectionism is a thing, I still often see them try to do too much at the one time. Often they know maps and models really well, and so obviously want to express their genius by layering the models into their writing. But the problem is, when you're trying to combine a Why Stack, with spiral dynamics, while talking to the avatar in the exact tone of voice while maintaining an equal balance between logic and emotion, you're probably trying to pull off too much at once.

If it's not already clear:

Perfectionsim is Dangerous

Especially when it comes to book writing.

So here's what to do about it.

1. Dump It – Then Refine It

The perfectionist wants it all to be pretty. Unfortunately, that's not how book writing works. Ask any creator, and they will tell you that their version 1.0 was a bit rough. But that's ok! Because there is a strategy that does work, though it will require you to temporarily suspend your need for it to be pretty.

The idea is to get to 65% complete as fast as possible. At 65% complete, what happens is the book becomes tangible, you can almost feel it, and it becomes so much more real than just an idea in your head. At 65%, you're on the final third, which is like the home stretch, and that in itself is inspiring.

To assist with this strategy, please refrain from writing a sentence then checking it. If you want your book to take 25 million years to write, then be my guest. But writing a sentence or paragraph, or even page, and then reviewing it and re-working it, is a sure fire way to slow you down.

The best practice strategy that we have found is to write for a big chunk of time, and THEN do a read through review.

One of our most productive book writers to ever join us on retreat, produced 75,000 words in 4 days by writing for a full day, then spending one hour at night reviewing. I'd recommend writing for at least one session (90 minutes) before reviewing, that way you can keep momentum.

Then, when it's all dumped out onto the page, you can then begin the refinement process.

2. You Don't Need To Write It In Chronological Order

Perfectionists sometimes think they need to start at the introduction and write chapters 1 through 10 in chronological fashion.

This is one way to write a book, but certainty not the only way.

What I'd recommend is firstly setting up the structural framework of your book first. Put in the parts, and the chapters headings within the parts, and if you've got any subheadings, put them in too. Essentially, you are setting up the skeleton of the fish.

Then, I encourage book writers to be guided by their intuition as to which section of the framework to create first.

For example, your first piece of writing that you create might be chapter 7. Similarly, you might write your introduction as the last piece you create. When you've got your structural framework set up from the beginning, it usually does not matter what order you create in.

3. Be Okay With Adding Layers

You don't make a layered chocolate mud cake just straight out of the oven.

First you bake the base.
Then you add icing.
Then you add another layer of cake.
Then more icing.

Then more cake.

And so on.

The same goes for book writing.

We had a health practitioner come to us to write a book a few years ago. On her first dump of the book, following the "get to 65% fast then refine method", her book was a little bit dry and logical. It was full of facts, and scientific terms. It lacked emotion, and didn't "feel" all that nice to read.

But that was totally fine.

Because in the baking of her book, she first needed a foundational layer of logic. It had to make sense. Then, her next layer was to refine the book, adding in more emotive words, making the writing "feel" nice to read.

She did that, and then went on to add a third layer – case studies and stories.

When her layering process was complete, she had a book that made sense, felt really good to read, and was alive with colourful stories and case studies that brought the points to life.

4. There's Perfection In The Imperfection

The rough and raw around the edges thing is often the most perfect. Let me give you an example.

At my high school graduation, the headmaster spoke, the school captain spoke, the parents, the prefects spoke too. They were all quite polished, as you would expect from a well-to-do private school graduation ceremony.

And then, Bob came to the stage. He barely passed year 12, and I think he failed English. He came up to the lectern, and stumbled on his way up. His tie was not done up properly, his shoe lace was undone, and his college shirt was hanging out over his pants. He was clearly not presenting the polished presentation that had proceeded the last 4 hours of ceremony.

Bob got up and told the story of how he had a tough childhood – his dad had walked out on him and his mum when he was 8. It effected Bob a lot, and he had thought about dropping out of school several times, because, it just all seemed so pointless. He spoke from the heart about times where his teachers pleaded with him to stay in school, and another time when he'd mucked up, and was going to be expelled from school, except for the fact that one of his teachers went into bat for him, arguing with the principal to let Bob stay in school.

He stumbled over his words, mispronounced heaps of them, and looked down for the majority of the talk. But through it all, he spoke from the heart, and there was not a dry eye in the house. Everyone was bawling, touched by the humanity of his message. He probably had a grade 4 command of English, but it was enough to captivate an entire audience of middle to upper class folks.

The moral of the story – raw and real and from the heart, will always captivate an audience more than a polished presentation.

Everyone has forgotten the 25 polished speakers that started the day.

But one thing is for sure – no one will EVER forget Bob.

Chapter 4
Publishing It

"I just want to rock up, do what I do best, and have the rest taken care of"

- The Creator and The Star

Who Can Help Me Publish? Arggh The Details!!

Finding the right team to help you with the publishing details can be a headache. You first need to learn all the terminology so you know what the hell you're talking about when it comes to publishing, and then you need to wade through a sea of different providers to find someone you trust. The reality is, that without quality help, there's every chance your manuscript will join the many manuscripts that have been resigned to a shoebox in a dusty closet.

This is not an encyclopedia of publishing so I won't include every small detail, but what I will do is layout your choices, so you can make the best decision about how to proceed.

The first fork in the road most people face is whether to go down the traditional publishing route, or self publish.

Let me lay it out for you super quick.

Traditional Publishing

(e.g. through a big behemoth publishing house like Hay House or Wiley or McGraw Hill)

Pros:

1. You get to say you were published by Hay House (seriously for some people this is a life dream).
2. The production quality of the interior and cover is professional

3. You may get pointed in the right direction regarding distribution, potentially nationally and globally into bookstores. This additional exposure can be valuable.

Cons:

1. They will likely edit and censor considerable parts of your work. If you believe in freedom of speech and authenticity of voice, then this could be a deal-breaker for you.
2. You don't have control over the price point – they do.
3. They take most of the cash: your royalties end up being quite low, perhaps $2 on a $20 sale of your book.
4. You probably won't retain creative control of the work.
5. This means it will be difficult to do updated versions, new offers in the back pages, and new calls to action when you launch new products.
6. The barrier to entry is considerable – they take on a limited number of projects each year, leaning heavily towards the books where the author already has an email list of 20,000 subscribers plus a big social media following.
7. It takes forever – 18 months would be considered fast.

Self-Publishing

Pros:

1. You have 100% freedom of speech, to own your voice and let rip with what you've got to say.
2. You get to keep 100% of all the royalties.
3. You control the price point.
4. The copyright and ownership of the work remains with you.
5. You can get your book to market FAST – in weeks rather than months or years.
6. There is no pre-requisite size of needing a following in order to publish.

Cons

1. Production quality can look cheap and tacky, tainting your professional image

Modern Hybrid Publishing

And then, there's what I call the **modern hybrid publisher** – this is what we are.

We take the best of traditional publishing, and the best of self publishing, to create a publishing experience that produces high production quality books while keeping you in the driver's seat regarding creative control, without requiring you to have a massive following to get started.

And you keep 100% of the royalties, and you can get it to market fast in weeks, not months or years, which means you can be bringing in leads and new business from your book fast!

A Word On Hay House

This is for those people hanging out to be published by Hay House. It's a worthy, admirable goal, and please keep them on your vision board – but please – do not let that dream stop you from publishing your book. I've spoke to many wonderful people who have so much to share, and could be helping so many people and making so many sales with their book, but they are holding off to publish with Hay House.

My suggestion to those people - get your book published anyway, and send Hay House a physical copy. It's much more tangible, and real, and shows them you are a serious contender. In terms of practical actions steps – choose to self publish, or else go with a modern hybrid publisher who doesn't lock you into a contract tying you exclusively to them.

At the Inspirational Book Writers, we don't lock our clients into only publishing through our publishing label, the SpiritCast Network. If you publish with us, and THEN get picked up by Hay House, good for you, we will send you on your way with our best wishes.

It's time to make a decision.

Which publishing path appeals most to you?

When considering your decision, be ok with the fact that you may take an alternative route to get to your destination (I'm talking to you Hay House folks). Realise that your book will make an impact on someone's life, regardless of where it is published.

Also be aware, that if you seek feedback from others on which decision to make, you will receive a million different answers.

At the end of the day, consider the information you have at hand, back yourself and make a decision.

Congratulations!

It's now time to celebrate – your message is on its way to the world.

Or is it?

Hold the Press!!
(The Ultimate Sabotage)

The boy stood at the gate to his tribe. He had never been beyond the gate, and had only heard rumours about what lay ahead. The thought of doing something new both terrified and excited him at the same time. He was poised on the precipice!

Often in the publishing process, I'm literally 2 minutes away from pressing print on the proof copies for a client, and I get a phone call, email, text message AND Facebook message:

HOLD THE PRESS!!

Despite having signed off the final approvals for their book, they want more changes. The requested changes can be big, or small, and are mostly inconsequential to the overall impact of the book. The craziest request I've received is from someone who emailed me wanting to add 12 new chapters to the book just moments before we pressed print!

Luckily, I've got a pretty good radar for what is a legitimate, necessary addition, and what is a stalling tactic. If it's legitimate and will make a positive impact on the overall book, we can make it happen. But mostly they are just stalling tactics.

You see, the final moment before pressing PRINT is a bit like the boy in the story above, about to take that leap into the new, though unknown exciting territory.

Will my current tribe reject me now I'm an "author"?

Who has got my back?

Will the next tribe accept me?

Where even is the next tribe?

Pressing PRINT, is the moment when it all becomes so much more real, it's the time to embrace the new journey.

I think the terrified excitement comes from moving up to the next level. At your existing level, you know your place. Potentially you're a big fish in a little pond. Potentially you're a little fish in a big pond. Whatever you're current location, publishing the book takes you to the next level, and changes things.

Any stalling tactics are merely a last ditch attempt to postpone the inevitable step up, and out, the writer knows they need to take.

So here are my top strategies for squashing sabotage.

1. Realise That The Second You've Finished, You've Already Learnt More

Most of the book writers I've worked with are humans that evolve and grow at a rapid rate. They are learning machines, and constantly upgrading and expanding their awareness.

So when a book writer comes to me with a "hold the press" moment, telling me they've learnt something new and need to put it in the book, I can understand how that's happened.

But here's the thing. Because you are constantly evolving, you are ALWAYS going to growing and evolving, in fact, 5 seconds after you hit submit on your manuscript, you are probably going to learn something new!

If you keep trying to get the new learnings in your book, you will keep postponing the release of your book. This is classic sabotage. It's like the boy in the story above, going to the gate of his village, having everything he needs to proceed, and then racing back to his home to pick up a new shoelace.

Cute, but not really effective!

The way to move past all of this nonsense is to remember that by saying yes to writing the book, you've already drawn the line in the sand. Your mission is to capture the learnings, and share your ideas to the best of your ability, up until the moment in history when you finished writing.

THAT is the line in the sand moment.

Any learning's beyond that point, can be saved for a revised edition in 12 months time, or for your next book.

2. Revisit Why You Started This Book Writing Journey

Sabotage often happens because the book writer is saturated in uncertainty of what the future holds, so they try to hold onto the certainty of the present moment. In these situations, take a deep breath, and refocus on your purpose.

What did you set out to achieve with this book? Review your goals, and reconnect to why you started in the first place. It was probably to share your wisdom and make an impact in peoples lives, or similar. By seeing the future you are stepping into, and gaining certainty around what that looks like, the desire to sabotage the next step often dissipates.

Remember that of course the future will be different – that's why you are doing it!

3. Give Yourself A Pat On The Back For Courageously Stepping Out

Have a little compassion for yourself. Zoom out, see where you've come from, and recognize what you've achieved thus far.

Breathe – and take the next step.

PUSH THE BUTTON!

It's time to bring it home.

The Strong Finish

"A 400m race, is not completed by running 396m"
— an athlete's proverb

Becoming complacent with a just few steps to go is bad news. It can cost you time and attention and open up an unnecessary can of worms of self doubt about your book. It's best just to hit it at pace, take the action and finish it!

You see, when the book is at 95%, the project is still open in your mind, taking up your valuable attention. When people say "oh it's hanging over my head", that's because it's consuming all their attention – attention that could be spent having fun travelling, spending time with loved ones, or building another piece of their business.

So, while becoming complacent might feel good in the moment, it quickly becomes burdensome. A nervous anxiety can set in, as the book writer starts to question everything.

"Have I done it right?" is a common question they ask themselves.

Stalling at 95% complete, the book writer becomes enthralled in reviewing and re-reading their work 100s of times. Let's be clear – review is a necessary part of creating a book. But mindless reviewing, is like scrolling Facebook – nothing more than mental masturbation.

However, I totally understand why the stall happens at 95%.

Firstly, a book is a creative expression. Thus, its not always clear what the finish point looks like. It's not like a sport, which has defined rules and

you know the game is over when the whistle blows. The tendency too, can be to hold on to your work, for fear of having missed something!

On top of that, some people are just not naturally good at finishing stuff. These people are typically creators or stars, who are incredible at starting!

You see, there are many, many details to take care of to pull together a book.

1. Calculating spine widths to the exact pixel, so the cover prints neat and snug on the spine
2. Matching the ISBN barcodes on the back cover to all the different versions of the eBook and paperback
3. Adding the Copyright page and relevant disclaimers.
4. Uploading the files in the correct format, complying with the retailers capitilisation requirements (trust me, you don't want to mess with iBooks – just do as they say – even if it's a bit weird!)
5. Setting up pricing across the world in different currencies
6. Selecting the right treaty exception so that 1) the United States IRS is happy and 2) so you don't pay them more than you are legally obliged to!

When you're a dynamic, ambitious high-achiever, you don't want to spend time learning this shit. You just want it handled, so you can continue making magic in your world.

So what can you do to finish strong in your book writing journey?

1. Keep Starting

It might seem weird that I'm saying "Keep Starting" while talking about finishing. But for some people, this is the exact strategy that will work wonders.

If you are a creator or star personality, naturally you will be excellent at starting things, and possibly not as naturally talented at completion.

One of our clients, Dane Tomas, is a Creator. He is always creating new stuff. When he writes his books, he frames each step along the way as "I'm starting".

When he gets towards the end of the book, he says "I'm starting chapter 12."

When he writes the conclusion, he says "I'm starting the conclusion."

When he does his final review, he says "I'm starting the review."

By framing everything as "start", he tricks himself into finishing.

2. Set A Finish Time Limit

A defined time for finishing compels completion. I see it sometimes on book retreat – the final 24 hours of writing are intensely productive and the participants often say things like "I'm coming in hot!" or "I'm on the home stretch!"

Give yourself a time limit, and stick with it.

3. Employ A Methodical Gap Analysis And Get Clarity On What Finished Looks Like

As mentioned above, sometimes it's hard to know when you are done.

To help you know when you are done, we use a tool called The Book Content Checklist to confirm all the relevant pieces are included in the book.

If you'd like to get a copy of the checklist for free, go to www.inspirationalbookwritersretreat.com.au/downloads to download your copy.

When you do your gap analysis, check-in in on the following questions:

- Is there anything I have missed?
- Have I hit my purpose?
- Have I done what I set out to do?
- Have I communicated what I wanted to communicate?
- In the tone that will match my audience?

4. Dial Up The Warrior Energy

This really comes from within. I believe that deep within each of us, there is a will power that can move mountains. It's the power that starts revolutions, creates change, and gets books done.

You might call it the Warrior, or the Beast, or Wonder Woman, or you might have some other archetypal character that inspires fierceness. Whatever it is for you, finishing a book requires a deep level of commitment and focus.

On the Inspirational Book Writers Retreat, we encourage everyone to have a power move that inspires strength and confidence and fire in their belly!

Combine this with your favourite music that gets you in the zone, and you have what it takes to finish the book.

Chapter 5
Launching It

"Anything can happen, if you let it" – *Mary Poppins*

The Spotlight

Writing a book can be like stepping onto the red carpet. If you're not ready for the limelight, it can be overwhelming.

That's because when you write a book, you are sharing your inner most thoughts, stories and ideas.

This can be quite vulnerable.

After 5 years of book coaching, I've heard writers say so many things.

I've listened to some of the most experienced health practitioners on the planet, tell me they feel nervous about exposing their work to the world.

I've seen multi-million dollar, self made businessmen question whether they deserve what's coming their way in terms of book launch success.

I've seen people sharing their inspirational life story, feel anxiety and fear at the prospect that people who knew them will read their work, and judge them.

The common thread is that launching a book brings up the fear of being seen. In everyday life, especially among high-achievers, we don't typically share our deepest innermost thoughts and beliefs and strategies.

We tend to wake up with a bang, put our superman cape on, and charge off to save the world! To infinity, and beyond!

So, to slow down, breathe in, get centred, and become intimate with your innermost thoughts, can be challenging in the writing process.

That's one thing.

The other thing is - are you ok with the spotlight?

You never know who is watching your book launch.

You never know who is watching that Top 100 Amazon Best-Seller List.

When your book launches, all eyes are on you, your message and your book!

For an introvert (defined as someone who prefers to recharge by themselves as opposed to in the company of others), it can be quite intense.

Now, some people are born for the stage! They love the limelight and for them, promoting the book is the easy part. But for the rest of us, we need to come to terms with the fact that we are, to some extent, exposing ourselves to the world stage.

1. Prepare To Be Witnessed In Your Vulnerability

The feeling of being exposed, or witnessed in your vulnerability, is often most felt by book writers sharing their "personal story with lessons" type book. Some people have been through some pretty tough life experiences. Recording them in a book that contains the hard won lessons can be a transformational experience, and indeed very healing.

We once worked with a beautiful human who had a dark past that many people knew about. The launching of that book was profoundly healing, as it was like a weight was lifted from her shoulders, now that the whole world had witnessed her story.

Business, leadership and how-to book writers can also experience a similar feeling, particularly if they are unveiling a new methodology or technique. It can be quite tender to show the world your creation, not knowing whether it will be accepted.

I recommend to all our book writers that they get a support crew around them for their launch night. There are usually plenty of people around who will be overjoyed to be part of a book launch, because after all – it's pretty exciting!

2. Love The Haters

You can't please all of the people all of the time. There are 7 billion people on this planet and many will not agree with what you say. This is totally fine, in fact it's a positive thing for the marketing of your book.

You want your book to be polarizing. You want people to decide to opt-in with passion, or opt-out if it's not for them. This is good news for you and your business, because the ones that opt-in with passion become raving fans, and the ones that opt-out mean you don't have to deal with pain in the ass customers.

The other thing to note, is that your book might emotionally trigger a reader. Everyone is on their own journey, and it is impossible to know what will or will not be a trigger for people.

For example, a few years back, one of our best clients released a brilliant book on coaching and personal development. It was a #1 Amazon best-seller across multiple categories and it really was the culmination of her life's work as a coach.

The day after she launched her book, she was scrolling Amazon to check for reviews. Among dozens of 5 star reviews, she was surprised to find a 1 star review. It was from a psychologist who only got as far as the copyright page of the book, before opt-ing out. This reader had read the disclaimer, taken offence to it, and quit reading the book on the spot! (for the record, it was a standard, completely normal disclaimer). No one will ever know what it was that triggered this reader, but clearly something did.

This type of thing will happen, especially if you've written a polarizing book, or one with swear words in the title or subtitle.

Can I Put Swear Words In My Title?

The simple answer is – of course you can – it is your book.

At the present moment in the book industry, using swear words in the title is very trendy, and many of the world's best selling books contain swear words in the title. I think that comes from a cultural phenomenon these days where people are really seeking raw and real wisdom, and they see swear words in the title as representing that. The other probably more obvious reason is that swear words gain the reading public's attention, and thus sell more books.

Ultimately, what it comes down to is, will your market resonate with your message?

If you are writing for a target market that is ok with swearing, or swearing is part of their everyday language, then sure, go for it, because it will likely help build rapport.

But if your market don't use swear words, e.g. it's a more family or children orientated market, then I would suggest don't use swear words.

If you do end up going with swear words, just be aware that it will trigger some people and they will probably tell you quite loudly that they disagree. If you are cool with that, then rock on!

3. Execute Your Launch Strategy

When you're launching your book and feeling all sorts of emotions, it can be really helpful to refocus on your launch strategy. If you just follow the strategy, you will get the result.

Going into detail on launch strategy is for another book, but if you'd like to download The Best-Seller Book Launch Strategy™ worksheet that we use with all our clients, then go to www.inspirationalbookwritersretreat.com.au/downloads to get your copy.

4. Pretend Like No One Is Watching!

This is a mindset hack I've used with book writers to great effect. Typically I'll suggest it in situations where the book writer is making a huge deal of their launch, it's become overwhelming and the anxiety sets in.

I define anxiety as looking into the future, seeing an undesirable result, and feeling anxious about it in the present moment, even before the thing has even happened. Often, the anxiety is about looking like a goose in front of other people.

What I've found, is that when you have that vision, and remove the people watching, the anxiety collapses, or at least lessens its grip.

Give it a go – and tell me how it works for you!

5. Schedule A Rest After The Launch

The spotlight can burn REALLY bright.

You've got your launch night, which might be online with thousands of people watching, or it might in a private book launch event at a local venue. There will likely be people sharing your book online, doing reviews on it, wanting you on their podcast, media appearances, speaking engagements – there's the opportunity to REALLY step onto the stage.

If you are someone who was born for the stage, this is probably your dream come true! If so, lap it up, it's your time to shine!

However, if you are more of an introvert, then it's a good idea to schedule a rest sometime after your launch. Look at your schedule and work out what fits best.

The Micro-Celebrity

One thing I've seen book writers squirm over is the idea of becoming a micro-celebrity. When you launch a book that is well-positioned, you literally become the person who "wrote the book on the thing". Put simply, you become THAT GUY or THAT GIRL in your space.

As the Ancient Hawaiian's would say, your book up levels your "Mana". Mana means power, influence, authority, prestige, and presence. So when prospects tell me they want to write a book for more authority and credibility, what I hear is they want to up level their Mana.

But Mana is not automatically conferred. It's not a transaction, like – write the book, get Mana. That's not how it works. To embody a deeper level Mana, of power, influence, authority, prestige and presence, you must own your power.

Own that you wrote a BRILLIANT BOOK.

Own that you have something of VALUE to OFFER the world.

Own that you have a level of INFLUENCE that allows you to MAKE AN IMPACT.

Because here's how you differ from the celebrities you may see in gossip magazines – you are using your newfound platform for LOVE, LEGACY and CONTRIBUTION. To further those ends, micro-celebrities, people with Mana, ask for, and take what they want from life.

So let's look at how this plays out when you launch your book. Let's start with 2 questions.

1. How comfortable are you with ASKING?
2. How comfortable are you with TAKING?

Because when you launch, you are ASKING people to buy your book. How comfortable are you with doing that? Even people with extensive sales backgrounds, who ask for the sale 100 times per day, have still had trouble with asking.

Here's some things you might have to ASK of people during the book writing journey:

1. Asking them for honest feedback
2. Asking to help you get unstuck
3. Asking people for testimonials, for forewords
4. Asking them to look after themselves for a week while you write the book! (Mums and Dads you know what I'm talking about!)
5. Asking them to buy the book
6. Asking them to share with their friends
7. Asking them to leave reviews
8. Asking them to buy bulk copies
9. Asking them to promote your book
10. Asking for moral support when you go to launch
11. Asking them to celebrate with you at your launch party

Book writing is a journey where your ASKING muscle will grow strong. You may be scared to ask, but I promise you, the answer is always no if you stay silent. So go ahead, ASK away, for this is the pathway to Mana, Micro-Celebrity and the authority you set out to obtain.

The TAKING muscle is the other muscle that grows strong over a book writing journey. From the moment you announce to the world you are writing a book, there are opportunities available for the taking.

Here's a stack of opportunities that are ripe for the taking:

1. Taking the opportunity to document the book writing journey. This can be hugely valuable for creating content that entices people to follow you. Photos, videos, little snippets of quotes

from your book – all of these can be used as social media content.
2. The opportunity for media and publicity, even before the book launches.
3. Taking speaking opportunities, and appearing on podcast worldwide.
4. Opportunity to do things a new way, re-work your funnel.
5. To open new conversations with people in your network – huge amounts of business can come from this.

Tall Poppy Syndrome

I couldn't write a section about Micro-Celebrity without addressing Tall Poppy Syndrome. Tall Poppy syndrome is especially prevalent in Australia. It is a social phenomenon in which people of genuine merit are resented, attacked, cut down, or criticised because their talents or achievements elevate them above or distinguish them from their peers[2].

When you tell people that you wrote a book, you will trigger all sorts of crazy reactions from people.

Some will say it's impossible!

Others will want to read it, and then proceed to tell you what's wrong with your book!

Their response can range from anything from a dull, non-responsive "meh" to a full on kick in the guts.

The solution:

1. Find A Community That Honours Your Success

What you're looking for is a community of people who you can share your successes with, celebrating the highs, sharing tips when it gets hard, and otherwise supporting each other.

---

[2] https://thingsaussieslike.wordpress.com/2014/11/12/no-18-tall-poppy-syndrome/

You want a community that is both high support – in that you are given the tools and connections to make your book happen – and high performance – in that the culture of the community is results focused.

To join for free our community of coaches, consultants, speakers, health practitioners and entrepreneurs supporting each other to write their inspirational books, go to: https://www.facebook.com/groups/inspirationalbookwriters/

2. Shine Brighter

In a world where tall poppy is prevalent, the best solution is to shine brighter. Just be SO good, SO giving, SO unquestionably brilliant in your shine that anyone who tries to cut you down is laughed out of town, because clearly you are a shining light.

Singer Kelly Rowland once said that her entire life and career transformed the moment she realized that she was God's gift to the planet. This was not said from a place of ego, rather, it was said from a place of knowing that what she has got to offer is valuable, and that she is a gift for the world to experience.

Own your inner rock star, and go shine brighter anyway!

3. Own Your Authority

When you write a book, you're asking people to agree with you, that you are an authority! Media can confirm this, but you have to own it first.

Are you ready for that?

Because if you can't own your authority first, then you can't ask them to agree to that, unless you own it first, so are you ready for that?

And remember, if you don't ask, the answer is always no.

The Rewards

You want to get a return on your investment from your book writing. Whatever the results are that you seek – whether it is new leads, next level authority, or even just to know you changed one person's life - books are like the golden handshake that gets you the red carpet treatment.

However, the worry is that you'll sink all this time into your book, and then you don't get what you want out of it.

The fear of failure in book writing shows up in a number of ways:

What if I can't finish my book?

What if no one turns up to my launch?

What if no one buys my book?

What if I don't make it to Amazon best seller?

And generally, what if I don't get the results I want?

If left unchecked, these thoughts can spiral a book writer into a dark pit of low-self esteem, crushing even crystal clear visions of success.

The other mistake I see book writers make is not clearly defining what they want from their launch. Without a clear vision of what success looks like for your launch, it's kind of like a rocket ship blasting off before the trip computer has been programmed with the destination. There's a whole lot of energy, but who knows where it is going?

So, what can we do about this?

1. Be Clear On The Purpose For Your Book

Authority & Credibility: as corny as it sounds, you can't spell Authority without Author. Building your authority is often the number one reason to write a book. People do business with people they know, like and trust. A well-positioned, best-selling book is like spending hours with a prospect, sharing your wisdom, values, beliefs and strategies via direct feed into their head.

When prospects are looking at whom they should work with, a published author will invariably be chosen over an expert who has not been published.

Program Sales: the big money from your book comes through what happens after the book launch.

You can make money off book sales, but its probably not going to buy you a yacht, though you might get a 6 week overseas holiday out of book sales if you've got a decent list.

The big money in books comes from selling your program AFTER the book launches.

Dane Tomas had great success with his book *Clear Your Shit*. After a highly successful book launch, Dane went on to sell $100,000 worth of his practitioner training programs in just 2 weeks following his launch. And keep in mind; this was for an event that was 6 months in the future. Pretty cool to sell out that far in advance!

If you'd like to learn exactly how he did it, go to www.inspirationalbookwritersretreat.com.au and download the $100K Case Study Video for free.

New Lead Generation: your book is a great tool to use as a lead magnet on your website.

You can set up the lead magnet in a couple of different ways. You can offer a couple of chapters of your book for free, or even the entire book in PDF in exchange for their email address.

You can put the link to buy your book in your email signature, so people you converse with on a regular basis are always seeing your work.

You can also set up a Facebook add funnel, offering your book for free of cheap if the prospect clicks through to your landing page.

You might have seen some of the big players in marketing and personal development do a free + shipping offer on the paperback version of their book.

Speaking Gigs And Book Tours: Books go hand in hand with a speaking career. When event organisers are looking to book talent for their event, conference or workshop, they will always choose a speaker who is published over one who is not. In fact, there are some stages where you won't even get a look-in if you haven't published a book.

Just ask 5 time Amazon best-selling author Jean Sheehan how her books have boosted her speaking career. She gets to pick and choose which gigs she does both nationally and internationally; such is the demand for her as a speaker.

Another incredible thing to do after publishing your book is to go on a Book Tour around the country, or even internationally. From Sydney to Dallas, from Prague to Auckland and back to Paris, we have had book writers launch their books all over the world to international audiences.

An outstanding example of a book tour is Glenn Munso, founder of the YouthYou Program in Melbourne, Australia. Glenn helps youth get off drugs through physical training and a strong mindset. When his book launched in the January of 2017, it kicked off a 12 month national tour, where he spoke at 40 + venues around the country, going to rural areas and doing talks inspiring change in each community. He sold thousands of books and has made a huge impact on the world.

Legacy And Impact: I love it when prospective book writers tell me they are writing their book because they want to leave their legacy. It gives me tingles of the best kind. Some of our book writers donate their book royalties to charities, and I love that this happens – I think it is important to give back.

Because I think that's what it's all about.

We are only here on earth for a short time, so we better make the best of it while we are here. And for those of us with families, wouldn't it be nice to etch your experiences into an actionable guide for people that walk the path after you.

I know money and credibility are great reasons to write a book, but sometimes its not about the stuff and things.

Sometimes, the knowledge that you were able to impact the life of even one human being is the most satisfying thing of all.

In the Inspirational Book Writers Program, we use a tool called The Book Purpose Builder™, which helps you to define the purpose for your book. If you'd like to access the short 10 minute video and worksheet for free, go to www.inspirationalbookwriersretreat.com.au/downloads

2. Be Clear On Your Evidence For Success

Now that you are clear on your main purpose for the book, it's time to get clear on your vision, and what success looks like for you. When you quantify and clarify exactly what you are aiming for, it sets you off on the path to success.

Ask yourself this question and then write the answers below. I've included a few results that you might want to adopt as your own.

What Results Do You Want?

- Amazon best seller
- Amazon reviews
- People emailing me saying how much it helped them
- Check my email and leads are flowing in off the book funnel
- My programs are filling up in advance with ideal clients
- I don't have to repeat myself anymore, because I can just say: "read my book!"
- Have my book as the ultimate business card – send it to clients, prospects and sell it at the back of the room at all speaking gifs
- I get invitations to events to speak

- Invitations to media appearances
- I do a podcast tour or media tour
- My prospects sign up at a rapid rate because the book has already prequalified them as good prospects
- I generate good will and reciprocity in the marketplace by giving away free copies
- I have some cool content from my launch party that builds my personal brand and reputation, such that people seek me out at a whole new level
- When out and about networking, people say to me "ohhh you're that guy that wrote XYZ"

3. Is Your Receiving Pipe Kinked?

Hmmm, I get that this one might seem a little strange at first, but stay with me.

The book writers we work with have a big heart, and are used to GIVING to their families, businesses, and clients. They take great pleasure in giving, and for many it's a strong, well developed part of their personality.

However once you've launched, you then begin to receive comments, reviews, purchases, enquiries, and new opportunities – it's all coming your way.

The question I like to ask every book writer, is how open are you to receiving the rewards that are coming your way? Because if your "receiving pipe" is kinked, you may miss the opportunities.

This could definitely be discussed in depth and at length at the campfire, but for now, I'll leave it there with the simple question for you to ponder.

4. Be Open To The Magic

Writing a book is an act of creation, much like building a house or giving birth to a baby. It is a labour of love, and a lot of emotional energy goes into its creation. That's why whenever a client begins the journey of writing a book, I invite them to be open to the magic of what could be.

I ask them, in your wildest dreams, what would you love to happen while creating this book? For many, it's a chance to dream again, as they reconnect to the possibilities that are always around us.

We've had book writers say they wanted to find love – and then 4 weeks after writing their book, meet their future husband.

We've had book writers want to be featured in documentaries – and 2 weeks after launching, be informed a national news network wants to do an entire documentary length feature on their business.

We've had writers say they want to get their book in the hands of Oprah – and their book ends up in the hands of Oprah's best friend! (close!)

The point is, writing a book is a chance to put the past to bed, reconnect to possibility and go to the next level in your life and business.

As my friend Nikki Fern says, "Keep room in your heart for the unimaginable magic."

The Next Level

"Only the butterfly can breakthrough its own cocoon"

Humans are an interesting species. We make our entire life so convenient and easy, and yet we thrive on challenge. We are driven by the need to be comfortable and certain, yet crave the adventure of new exciting endeavors.

We are a walking contradiction, and yet, deeply wired in our DNA is the desire to grow and evolve. The feeling of progress is what makes humans happy, because then we are satisfying the primal blueprint that says "do more, be more, give more".

The sad thing is, many people get locked into comfortable patterns. Even the people we work with, leaders in their fields, still sometimes get too comfortable.

Writing a book is the perfect antidote.

The process of writing a book, challenges every sense of your humanity. You'll come face to face with the best and worst parts of your personality, and your vulnerabilities will be tested. Putting yourself out there, especially around something that you, and only you have created, is a noble, and admirable step.

If you didn't put your words out into the world, the world wouldn't evolve, and problems would continue to exist. It has been said that the greatest injustice happens when good people stay silent during moments when they should have spoken up. I believe that is true.

We CAN change the world with our words.

And it starts, by you changing YOUR world.

When you step up and out and become a leader, you become an example of what is possible for others. You become a lighthouse, like a beacon of light for those needing guidance, wisdom, intuition and solutions. By helping yourself, you help others. And trust me, the world is DESPERATE for positive role models right now.

All your trials and tribulations have led you to this point. You've been through the tough stuff, stormed through the fire and had your heart cracked open more times than you care to remember. It's installed in you, the learning, wisdom and understanding that can only be earned the hard way through direct personal experience.

And now it's time to put that hard-won wisdom to good use. To write a book, where you can pass on your knowledge to others for generations to come, so that they too may know how to solve their problems and raise their consciousness.

Only YOU can write YOUR book, and now, it's time.

May the wisdom in this book, assist you in your onward book writing journey.

I look forward to reading your book.

Best regards,

Dave Thompson
Founder, Inspirational Book Writers Retreat

About Dave Thompson

Dave Thompson is a 5 time Amazon best-selling author and the founder of the Inspirational Book Writers Retreat.

The program is famous for taking coaches to paradise for a week to write their book, and publishing them 6 weeks later.

As of 2018, his WRITE – PUBLISH – LAUNCH methodology has seen more than 60 authors and 75 books published, including more than 50 Amazon best-sellers.

Known affectionately as "King Coconut", Dave is renowned for his island-style hospitality, fun, humour and warrior-style results driven focus.

To get in contact, email him at dave@livingoutrageously.com

The Book Map Game Plan Session

"Map out your entire book plan in 90 minutes, and save yourself potentially years of false starts, by starting on the right foot."

WHAT IS IT?

The Book Map Game Plan Session is a 90 minute session, 1:1 with Inspirational Book Writer's Founder Dave Thompson.

HOW IT WORKS

In this power packed session, you will:

- Discover your personal strategy for creativity and productivity (this is SO important for beating procrastination and building flow)
- Get clear on your purpose for the book (no more wasting time on false starts heading in the wrong direction)
- Get clear on your vision and what success looks like for you (there's so many things you can do with a book – let's get clarity on exactly what is important to YOU.)
- Dial in your message (title and sub-title) so that it's powerful and compelling, and stands out from the crowd.
- And create a structure that both feels good and makes sense for your book.

Dave will record book map notes, and send them to you at the end of the session. You are welcome to record the session if you wish.

To find out more, go to:

http://www.inspirationalbookwritersretreat.com.au/the-book-map-game-plan-session/

PUBLISH + LAUNCH Program

WHO IT'S FOR

This program has been specifically designed for coaches of all types, practitioners, consultants, speakers, experts, personal brands and entrepreneurs who already have a manuscript (or are nearly complete) and want help tying it all together, publishing it, and launching to #1 Amazon Best-Seller and beyond.

DO WHAT YOU DO BEST

You've written the book! Congratulations! But the hardest part is yet to come. Not knowing how to publish it has left so many manuscripts floundering in dusty hard-drives, never seeing the light of day. What a waste!

You could spend weeks and weeks doing it yourself, trying to figure out how to publish your book in a confusing publishing industry that has just as many exceptions as it does general rules. Save yourself the headache, and let us take care of your book project, so you can focus on what you do best.

It's time to capitalise on the momentum you've created and commence publishing, and launching your book.

To find out more, go to www.inspirationalbookwritersretreat.com.au/publish-launch-program

The Inspirational Book Writers Retreat

Come to paradise for a week, and be published 6 weeks later

Our promise has always been that simple.

This event has been specifically designed for coaches of all types, practitioners, consultants, speakers, experts, personal brands and entrepreneurs who want to come to paradise for a week, and leave with a completed manuscript.

We know life is busy, but we also know you can spare a week in paradise to finally complete that one goal that just won't go away – that of writing your book.

This is the event for you if you absolutely cannot procrastinate any longer and just…

Want to Get it Done

Writing a book is one of the hardest things in the world to do on your own. You're an incredibly capable human and could do it, but why not just get some help? We have a 100% success rate for people who follow our book writing process.

Places on retreat are by application only.

To apply and find out more, go to www.inspirationalbookwritersretreat.com.au

Contact Us

Website: www.inspirationalbookwritersretreat.com.au

Facebook: www.facebook.com/IBWRetreat

Instagram: www.instagram.com/inspirationalbookwriters

Email Dave directly: dave@livingoutrageously.com

Notes

Notes

Notes

Notes

Notes

Notes

Notes

Notes

Notes

Notes

Notes

www.ingramcontent.com/pod-product-compliance
Lightning Source LLC
Chambersburg PA
CBHW020442220526
45464CB00002B/825